ENVIRONMENTAL
ISSUES

BookLife

By Gemma McMullen

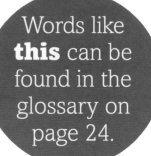

Words like **this** can be found in the glossary on page 24.

Book Life
King's Lynn
Norfolk PE30 4LS

ISBN: 978-1-78637-019-8

All rights reserved
Printed in Malaysia

©This edition was published in 2018.
First published in 2016.

Written by:
Gemma McMullen

Designed by:
Matt Rumbelow

A catalogue record for this book
is available from the British Library.

CONTENTS

WHAT IS A HABITAT?

A habitat is the place where an animal lives. Almost every place on Earth is a habitat. Many different animals live in the same habitat. They rely on plants and each other for food. Animals' bodies are suited to the habitat in which they live.

WHY ARE HABITATS IN DANGER?

Habitats all over the world are being destroyed. Humans are destroying habitats by mistreating them or by taking them over for their own use. The number of animals living inside endangered habitats is getting smaller and some species have even become **extinct**.

THE RAINFOREST

Rainforests are large areas of forest that are warm and wet. The trees of a rainforest are very tall and close together. Most of the world's rainforests are tropical. This means that they get a large amount of rainfall and the plants stay green all year.

Rainforests are home to over half of all of the animal species that we know about, including monkeys, birds, bats and butterflies.

DID YOU KNOW THAT NEW ANIMAL SPECIES ARE BEING DISCOVERED ALL THE TIME?

THE MOUNTAIN GORILLA

Mountain gorillas live in thick, misty rainforests, high up in the mountains. They can only be found in Africa and there are not many left. Mountain gorillas cannot be helped by zoos because they do not survive in them.

One of the reasons that the number of mountain gorillas has become so small is that for a long time they were hunted by people. More recently, their habitats have been cut down for extra farming land. The **remaining** gorillas live in protected parks where **rangers** work hard to keep them safe.

THE OCEAN

Almost three-quarters of the world's surface is covered in salty water. There are five main oceans, the Pacific Ocean being the largest. The oceans are extremely important. They even affect the weather. Below the oceans, minerals and oil can be found.

Oceans are home to some of the largest and the smallest creatures on the planet, including whales, dolphins, sea turtles and fish.

DID YOU KNOW THAT THOUSANDS OF BIRDS RELY ON THE OCEANS FOR THEIR FOOD?

THE BLUE WHALE

Whales are large mammals that live in the sea. There are 83 species of whale in the world. Blue whales are the largest of all the whales. Blue whales can be found in deep oceans all over the world.

More than half of young blue whales die because they are not strong enough to swim in rough water or they are killed by orcas. People used to hunt blue whales, which has meant that numbers have become low.

AN ORCA

POLLUTION IN THE OCEAN IS A DANGER TO WHALES TOO.

THE AFRICAN SAVANNAH

A savannah is a large area of grassland. Savannahs have large amounts of trees, but, unlike forests, the trees are scattered around. There are two seasons in the African savannah; the dry season and the wet season.

Many animals can be found living on the plains of Africa, including giraffes, zebras and cheetahs. During the dry season, these animals can struggle to find water and must be careful to avoid waiting crocodiles!

PLANTS LIVING IN A SAVANNAH MUST BE ABLE TO WITHSTAND LONG PERIODS WITHOUT WATER TO SURVIVE.

THE AFRICAN ELEPHANT

The African elephant is the largest animal on land. There are two types of African elephant, the savannah elephant being the largest. Elephants need a large amount of space. They can **roam** areas of up to 30,000 square kilometres.

The population of African elephants has largely **decreased**. Some people choose to kill elephants for their ivory tusks. These people are called poachers. Ivory is used to make jewellery and can be ground down to make medicine.

TUSKS

POACHERS SELL THE IVORY IN ORDER TO MAKE MONEY. ELEPHANTS' MEAT AND SKIN ARE ALSO SOLD.

THE ARCTIC

The Arctic is located in the most northern part of planet Earth, making it very cold. Much of the area is covered in thick ice, depending on the time of the year. The Arctic is made up of the Arctic ocean and parts of Canada, Russia, the USA, Greenland, Norway, Finland, Sweden and Iceland.

Despite its low temperatures, the Arctic is home to many species of wildlife, including polar bears, walruses, seals and whales. There are even some people who live in the Arctic. These people are called Inuits.

DID YOU KNOW THAT INUITS HAVE ADAPTED THEIR LIVES TO SURVIVE IN THE COLDEST AREA OF OUR PLANET?

THE POLAR BEAR

The polar bear is a close relative to the brown bear. The polar bear lives in the Arctic, and, although it is born on land, spends much of its life on the sea ice. Polar bears are **carnivorous**, mainly eating seals and fish.

For some time, polar bears were hunted by humans, which led to a large decrease in numbers. Now they are protected. The largest threat to polar bears is climate change. As the world gradually warms up, the ice of the Arctic melts, leaving the polar bear with less of a habitat in which to hunt. Pollution is another threat to polar bears.

OTHER ENDANGERED ANIMALS

Unfortunately, there are many other animals on our planet that are also at risk.

There are only a few black rhinos left. They mostly live in Western Africa. They are largely in danger due to poachers killing them for their horns.

The snow leopard is being hunted for it's rare, beautiful fur. It's numbers are now near disappearing.

Many of the forests where orangutans live have been made into farms. There have also been **severe** forest fires, which have made life for orangutans very difficult.

The northern bald ibis almost vanished from Europe completely in the 17th century because people hunted it for food.

GLOSSARY

carnivorous	an animal that only eats meat
decreased	made fewer in amount
extinct	a species of animal no longer alive
rangers	people who work to protect an area of land
remaining	still existing
roam	wander freely over a wide area
severe	serious or very great

INDEX

Photocredits: Abbreviations: l–left, r–right, b–bottom, t–top, c–centre, m–middle.
All images are courtesy of Shutterstock.com.
Front Cover – fotoslaz. 1 – Eric Isselee. 2, 6 – Stephane Bidouze. 3, 24 – David Carillet. 4 – Eduard Kyslynskyy. 5 – Martin Haas. 7 – Darren Baker. 8 – bimserd. 9 – Palenque.10 – Ase. 11 – Rich Carey. 11onset – Benjamin-Nocke. 12 – Seb c'est bien. 13 – 4Render. 13inset – WvdMPhotography. 14 – E. O.. 15 – Maggy Meyer. 16 – Donovan van Staden.17 – 2630ben. 18 – Denis Burdin. 19 – bikeriderlondon. 19inset – Christopher Wood. 20 – La Nau de Fotografia. 21 – FloridaStock. 22bl – Four Oaks. 22r – andamanec. 23b – Edwin Butter. 23t – Stanislav Fosenbauer.